THE INCLINATION TO MAKE WAVES

poems

Hilary Sideris

The Inclination to Make Waves
©2016, Hilary Sideris
ISBN: 978-1-937806-07-1
Big Wonderful Press, LLC
Brooklyn, NY

Design by Big Wonderful Press
All Rights Reserved

Grateful acknowledgment is made to the following journals where these poems have appeared or are forthcoming:

The Baltimore Review: "What," "Flat"
Barrow Street: "Crow," "Work"
Big City Lit: "Blot," "Even"
Confrontation: "Blow"
The Country Dog Review: "Moll," "Boon"
Ducts: "Miss," "Jilt," "Warp"
Fogged Clarity: "Boss"
Forge: "Ford"
Green Mountains Review: "Good," "Move," "Mute"
The Midwest Quarterly: "Mine"
The Laurel Review: "Gift," "Host"
Natural Bridge: "Lure"
The Normal School: "Bass"
Pagan Friends: "Leek"
Salamander: "Mate," "Pass"
The Same: "Cute," "Fine," "Glen," "Mind," "Wake," "Tear"
Spillway: "Dust," "Bond"
The Southern Poetry Review: "Mole," "Pill"
Qwerty: "Debt," "Hand," "Sock"
Tar River Poetry: "Fork"
Third Wednesday: "Leaf," "Stay"
The Tower Review: "Tact"
West Branch: "Bend," "Sage," "Said"

Contents

GOOD	5
MOVE	6
FLAT	7
BOND	8
GLEN	9
VASE	10
LURE	11
DEBT	12
BASS	13
EVEN	14
BOSS	15
MATE	16
PASS	17
MUTE	18
FORK	19
BLOW	20
LEAF	21
MOLL	22
HAND	23
BEND	24
SAID	25
LEEK	26
FORD	27
CUTE	28
HOST	29
CROW	30
BOON	31
JILT	32
TACT	33
FINE	34
WAKE	35
DUST	36
MIND	37
SOCK	38
PILL	39

BLOT	40
WHAT	41
MISS	42
GIFT	43
TEAR	44
HANG	45
MOLE	46
STAY	47
OATH	48
WARP	49
WORK	50
MINE	51
SAGE	52

GOOD

Report card B, commodity,
food long in the fridge,

unspoiled. Antonym and origin
of evil, grade of kisser

in the kissed mouth's mind.
The news I'm leaving,

you decide what kind, what
for, assign the qualifier:

pretty, very, no. You
never had it so.

MOVE

What woolens do
slowly in summer, planets

around suns, tearjerkers
and homewreckers: cause,

arouse, sell merchandise.
There'll be no more dwelling

on eviction. Even at a loss,
now everything must go.

Wise, to hire a lawyer.
Smooth, across a dance floor.

Meaning of excuse me
on a rush-hour train.

FLAT

It got too smooth, too
even, but we lacked

the inclination to make
waves. Across a range

of frequencies, it stayed
the same, below true

pitch in song. It was
one story in a house.

I lived with you.
It went like that.

BOND

Handshake, shackle,
contract, kiss, a man's

word in a gone man's
world, a spy's idea

(cuts into his skin,
digs out the bullet)

of duty: don't orphans
make the best recruits?

No chaser like the past.
I never liked this place,

he shrugs, his boyhood
home in flames.

GLEN

He sings her open,
Gaelic green, supine,

a valley yielding
her clear cleavage, easy

on the eye, the mind.
He strums a river

between her hillsides,
his sleeping bag

rolled up and stashed
behind her sky.

VASE

As a girl I never
saw the image

in reverse, of lovers
face to face, only

the space between
them, vaguely

woman-shaped,
elegant neck

filled with wild
flowers, set on

a table in case
of a guest.

LURE

Decoy on a long cord,
artificial bait, seduction's

iridescent tool. Draw with
a promise of pleasure or gain

away from the orderly course.
Antonym: repel. He said he'd

never cared for anyone he felt
desire for, and remained

a rake and stranger, fling,
affair. Sign of fire through

darkening cloud, red
flag, clear and lurid.

DEBT

Onus that won't
roll over, owned

up to, written down,
synonym of sin,

hump, summit to
surmount. Balance due,

in ancient nations
paid in slavery, or did

you say in your thick
sexy accent, death?

BASS

From arcane *buss*, archaic
cuss, akin to Middle English

kissen, you descend from niche
to trench, darker to darkest,

fat-lipped and low-pitched.
Striped in a lake, at sea

spiny-finned, blacken in my
cast-iron pan, lobster eater

from the rocky bottom,
my large mouth's deep dish.

EVEN

I lied saying I loved
you wholly, craved

in hindsight maybe
half, leftover from

slaughter, laughter
splitting me and my big

mouth. Who's to say
who I played, whether

left or leaver better,
cleaver to you, cleft

in two, both equal,
neither enough.

BOSS

Could I labor better,
repress my yes hiss

in the power of a higher
wage, a multitasking

tongue, a sticky kiss
in the Employees Only

pantry over free cookies?
Can you breathe life

into me, mortal to whom
I submit my report,

by whom I'm blessed
when I sneeze.

MATE

Homebody, my chain
and ball, mannish boy

to my womanish girl,
son of a gun to my mother

of pearl, dark one I know so so.
Knife to my sheath, my vessel's

skipper, my hussy's hussar,
barbarian to my Greek,

pillar and pillager
of my house, I espouse.

PASS

The bar, the buck, Saint Peter's
gate, with flying colors,

for normal or straight. Creole,
mulatto, octoroon, fair enough

to get in and gain a title like Queen
of the Demi-Monde for a gal

who'll hustle and play in tune,
for a man: Did he ramble?

Could he blow? Knew how
to swing till they laid him low,

shot him down, out of this
world, *on*, Lord, *away*.

MUTE

Mutt was the first to choke
his horn, stuck a rum glass

in the bell and swung.
No high-note player to rival

Armstrong, he stayed in his
range and made it moan.

You heard every chord, muffled
but lush, and the drummer's

sandpaper, back before
the wire brush, saying *shhh*.

FORK

Who first had the sharp
idea to scoop as well

as spear, upgrade from tool
to silverware? Upheavals ago,

in ducal circles, three fingers
seemed unseemly, five uncouth.

Upturned, New-World style
or in Continental fashion,

tines curved down, shut up
and put it in your mouth.

BLOW

Caught off the Korean coast,
after the golden frog, you're

the most dangerous, delicious
vertebrate. Caging you's not

enough: you need your mouth
stitched shut, liver & ovaries

cut out. A pinhead's worth
of puffer powder fells a man;

highly diluted, dulls his pain.
No antidote. Those who drink

your soup, they say, are stupid
in Japan, as are those who don't.

LEAF

I never knew how
London Plane differed

from Sycamore, how both
resembled Sugar Maple

in their lobes, how Black
Mangrove compared to

Mountain Laurel's untoothed
edge, as hard to tell apart

as Sassafras and Water Oak,
until I thumbed the pages

of this Audubon tree book
from Amazon, pre-owned

by someone named Sue
Moore, who smoked.

MOLL

Dollface, dame,
molly coddle,

decoy to mollify
Officer Doyle, poor

pretty girl lured
by finer things, hear-

sayed, defamed.
Reader, herein

lie lurid details,
all but her name.

HAND

for Lynn

My friend meant heart
when she said, *Isn't*

*there a poem you know
by hand?* She'd seen,

on a park bench that day,
a girl giving a boy (how

else to say?) a handjob,
and a toddler triking by

in a dream that recurs,
the image and the word.

BEND

Just as the word
is mostly end,

we've reached the path
where brittle leaves

crack underfoot,
and we admit it's late

for flexibility, for faith
that we can break

so many times
and mend.

SAID

You didn't ask,
I didn't tell

about my day,
then it was days

we didn't speak.
You pointed out

this wasn't good
and I agreed,

although I had
nothing to add.

LEEK

On a field so green
it seemed blue, Saxon

battled Celt. Smart
soldiers steered clear

of the darker, bitter end.
Nero chewed the blanched

bulb, the chartreuse,
Vichyssoise stem and hula

fringe, but couldn't mend
his madness or marriage.

FORD

Four cylinders in a solid
block, suspended by

semi-elliptic springs,
800 dollars in 1908

Detroit, driving the un-
skilled workers' wage

against the customer's
right always, so long

as he wants his Model
T black, the fastest

color, by seven
seconds, to dry.

CUTE

I once was, and so, sister,
were you, but at the time

we didn't know—a law
of nature and low

self-esteem. Our mother
was beautiful, and like

the Renaissance artists,
considered beauty a virtue,

a point she dwells on
still, however moot.

HOST

I pardon my
son, I know it's

hard to have
a lodger in your

house, scarfing
your eucharist

wafers, and even
harder when

your guest is
flesh and blood.

CROW

User of tools,
born charlatan,

black swagger
on blue tarpaulin,

carrion eater,
glossy in the almost

human dawn, beak
in the eye, shrill

cry between
betrayals.

BOON

Blessing, bonus,
stroke of luck, boom

in the boondocks
where you in boots

and bearskin blaze,
where there are

trails already, paths
you can't see,

taking beauty
for booty.

JILT

Juliet, Jillian,
harlot Jill,

in French *jillet*,
the flirt, unfeeling,

felt, who flung her
don into the dirt,

having fanned
his flame,

the abrupt slut
who ended it.

TACT

I didn't put it
that way,

in those terms
exactly,

can't say
with precision

how it went,
but thought we

tacitly agreed
to split the rent.

FINE

If you ask how
I am, do I go on

or answer in one
word at the film's

end, pronounce
my English *I*,

diphthong without
umlaut, my silent

e, as if to say
I can't complain?

WAKE

Pain keeps us up.
At two and four we

take our pill for back
and head, respectively,

wonder why us, how
long will this go on,

where do we rate them
on a scale of one to ten,

your sharp pang,
my dull ache?

DUST

Eyelash, hangnail,
household cloud,

swept up, broken
down. Near dusk

on a brown page
of definitions. Six

layers of skin. Husk
of someone I will

have been. Devil,
jacket, bunny, bin.

MIND

I like the word best
as a verb, as in,

do you, would you
rather not hear

my dream of you
with Alzheimer's?

I said I did
until you stopped.

Then we feigned
sleep until we slept.

SOCK

One's on. The other
can't be found. *Cazzo,*

more snow! New York's
a winterfucker, but

you talk as if you
think I cleaned it up.

Check both your boots.
Do you want me

to ask you not to go?
Don't you have to?

Eccola, in your coat
pocket. *Allora, addio.*

PILL

Sleep, just
let me skim,

not understand
your page, my

estranged tongue,
leave me a clean

margin, a leaf to turn,
words wavering.

Make this torn sky
kind against my will.

BLOT

Ammonia for chocolate,
aspirin for sweat,

lemon and tartar
for rust, meat tenderizer

for blood. For grease,
more grease works best.

From pinstripe, herringbone,
seersucker in summer,

tropical wool: I'll follow
instructions closely

to remove you, and,
halfway, I will.

WHAT

Today I called the kettle
a bottle, my daughter

by my sister's name.
I stumbled over antic,

how it's almost antique,
reached in my deep

purse for what do you
call it, lipstick, toothpick,

mint? Not as I thought,
but how I meant.

MISS

Much as I've
failed, for all

I lack, alone as I
may look without

the phone I left
home, bring me

more wine, nice
man, and please

don't call
me that.

GIFT

Poison in German,
it still eats at you,

the luxury sheet set
I bought, one thousand

threads, but not cotton.
Nor will I forget

the diamond studs
I mentioned in my

subtle way, the ones
you didn't buy.

TEAR

It makes me wild,
the reckless way

you open envelopes,
boxes, pick scabs,

pile up scraps.
I never know how

to pronounce you,
small but volatile

word, to rip you
into shreds or sob.

HANG

Again, at dawn,
you buckle the belt,

close the curtain.
Not even drink

numbs the noose
rubbing. Still, you

have to kick to fall
into the thick

tightening of time
around the neck.

MOLE

Black mark
on my pale neck,

no matter how
small and

inconspicuous,
your dark

drills down,
blind animal

or secret
agent sent

to infiltrate
cells.

STAY

Just as you are,
may you go on,

under the sway
of sound, long

vowel pounding
the sand, call it

a wave, wait for
one more. Don't

get up, don't jot
down what it

meant. But if
you do, don't go.

OATH

You tempt
me sometimes

to explain why
our pact broke,

out of desire
to paragraph,

bullet point,
persuade you,

but by God
I won't.

WARP

Your limber twist,
your cocky slalom,

swivel, pivot, pirouette,
how did they turn

into a skewed shuffle
across a crooked room?

In this humidity,
the door won't close.

You stoop to tie
huge shoes.

WORK

Operate, seduce, bestir.
Mulish, bred to bear.

Like a dog, wagging
to be of use. Nails chewed

in a cubicle. For god, boss,
off the books or clock,

freighted or fraught.
Just to get out of the house,

what do you do? What
have you wrought?

MINE

Go your way,
extract your

ore, your haul
as rich, your

well as deep
or deeper than

the cave I am
all of. Go on,

alloy of my
dark joy.

SAGE

I've lived long
enough to cultivate

these silvered
leaves, to pluck what

uses wisdom has, to prune
my *salvia* in spring,

savoring age, the not
unpleasant sting

of being healed,
not saved.

www.ingramcontent.com/pod-product-compliance
Lightning Source LLC
Chambersburg PA
CBHW021453080526
44588CB00009B/825